GREAT EXIT PROJECTS ON THE
VIETNAM WAR
AND THE
ANTIWAR
MOVEMENT

GREAT SOCIAL STUDIES EXIT PROJECTS™

GREAT EXIT PROJECTS ON THE
VIETNAM WAR
AND THE
ANTIWAR
MOVEMENT

Carolyn DeCarlo

rosen publishing's
rosen central®

New York

Published in 2020 by The Rosen Publishing Group, Inc.
29 East 21st Street, New York, NY 10010

First Edition

Library of Congress Cataloging-in-Publication Data

Names: DeCarlo, Carolyn, author.
Title: Great exit projects on the Vietnam War and the antiwar movement / Carolyn DeCarlo.
Description: New York: Rosen Publishing, 2020 | Series: Great social studies exit projects | Audience: Grades 5–8. | Includes bibliographical references and index.
Identifiers: LCCN 2018021612| ISBN 9781499440492 (library bound) | ISBN 9781499440485 (pbk.)
Subjects: LCSH: Vietnam War, 1961–1975—United States—Juvenile literature. | Vietnam War, 1961–1975—Psychological aspects—Juvenile literature. | Vietnam War, 1961–1975—Protest movements—United States—Juvenile literature. | Draft—United States—Juvenile literature. | Peace movements—United States—History—20th century—Juvenile literature. | United States—Politics and government—1963–1969—Juvenile literature.
Classification: LCC DS558 .D43 2020 | DDC 959.704/31—dc23
LC record available at https://lccn.loc.gov/2018021612

Manufactured in the United States of America

CONTENTS

INTRODUCTION

Middle school curricular standards have grown to encompass the need for project-based learning, a skill with which students will become very familiar as they create their own social studies exit projects. Middle school exit projects—or, more narrowly, the eighth-grade exit project—encourage students to develop knowledge in a specific topic by asking questions and learning more about that topic than they might just from studying the general curriculum. This inquiry, or question-based, process is driven by students' own production and presentation of material, rather than from instruction relayed by teachers or other professionals. These projects require students to use creative and critical thinking together to keep their audience interested during their presentation. They also must maintain a connection to the real world, through analysis of authentic problems and issues. Combining these skills is designed to demonstrate mastery over a curricular subject as a middle school student before continuing to the demands of high school course work.

Spanning almost two decades, the Vietnam War (1954–75) and its opposing antiwar movement was an important period in American history, and provides a worthy topic of study for an exit project. Begun as part of a larger regional conflict known as the Indochina Wars, American involvement in the war dates back to the Truman administration when economic and military aid was first provided to prevent the spread of communism into then-French ruled Vietnam. After the French deserted, Vietnam split into the communist North and anticommunist South, with communist supporters known as Viet Cong remaining an active

Young American men were sent to fight in Vietnam during the war, with combat troops entering the country in 1965.

presence in the South. US military advisers, present in small numbers in the 1950s, were introduced into South Vietnam on a larger scale beginning in 1961, with active combat units mobilized by President Johnson in 1965. By the beginning of President Nixon's term in office in 1969, more than 500,000 US military personnel were stationed in Vietnam. Countering this military involvement was a burgeoning group of pacifist (meaning peaceful) objectors to the war, whose protests were numerous and well-heard. From this antiwar movement, a counterculture known as the hippies emerged, maintaining an active presence in the United States well into the 1970s.

Project-based learning is an instructional strategy that allows students to pursue knowledge as it pertains to their own interests, and to demonstrate their findings through a variety of presentation modes. Students will read through a number of engaging and investigative social studies projects related to the Vietnam War and the antiwar movement, which can be used as models for their own project. They will be expected to create and develop their own projects, and not merely copy an idea found in this text. Project-based learning very much emphasizes the importance of brainstorming and cultivating one's own ideas as students prepare to enter the demands of high school study.

CHAPTER ONE

ADVANCING THE TIMELINE

At its core, studying history involves the evaluation of why events occur and how developments unfold in the way that they do. This kind of study relies on a deep understanding and evaluation of continuity and change within a focused lens, such as location. By creating a framework for a historical era, the scholar may examine this period from different positions

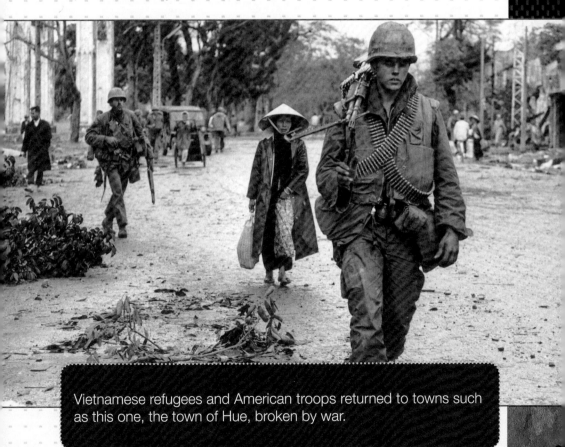

Vietnamese refugees and American troops returned to towns such as this one, the town of Hue, broken by war.

in time, and from multiple points of view. The study of history necessitates a high degree of chronological reasoning that involves connection, causality, significance, and context.

Historically, the Vietnam War and antiwar movement can be used to mark a period of open unrest in American history, where between the fear of communism, manifested in the Cold War, and open discussion and protestation of social evils such as racism, sexism, and other national injustices, leading to the civil rights movement, lack of support for the war in Vietnam would come as no surprise at home. Linking these social and political movements together as visible indicators of the same surging attitudes of unrest and unhappiness amongst the general public is an important step to understanding the historical context of the Vietnam War and its opponents in the antiwar movement.

PRESIDENTIAL PROFILE: LYNDON B. JOHNSON (1908–1973)

Elected in 1960 as Vice President to running mate President John F. Kennedy, President Johnson was sworn into office after Kennedy's assassination on November 22, 1963. His desire was to achieve a "Great Society" for the American people while in office, which he quickly proved first by obtaining a new civil rights bill and a tax cut. Johnson was reelected by the American people in 1964 by the widest popular margin in American history. Johnson's Great Society program of 1965 included: aid to education; Medicare; urban renewal; conservation; a wide-scale fight against poverty, crime, and delinquency; and guaranteeing the right to vote for all Americans.

His achievements were numerous, including the 1965 Medicare amendment to the Social Security Act, but largely overshadowed by two overriding crises gaining force in America: continued racial unrest at home, and continued fighting in Vietnam spurred by his own involvement in the Gulf of Tonkin Resolution and subsequent introduction of combat troops to the area. Choosing to withdraw his candidacy for reelection in 1968, Johnson did not live to see peace in his nation.

Soon after being sworn in, President Lyndon B. Johnson found himself greeting the nation on his first televised Thanksgiving Day program from the executive office of the White House.

QUESTION 1 HOW AND WHEN DID THE VIETNAM WAR, ALSO KNOWN AS THE SECOND INDOCHINA WAR, BEGIN IN VIETNAM?

Despite being known in Vietnam as the American War, or the War Against the Americans to Save the Nation, the war began long before American involvement. In this drawn out conflict over political policy and communism in the country, the government of South Vietnam fought against communist rule in North Vietnam and its allies, known as the Viet Cong, in the South. The war was also tied to a larger regional conflict known as the Indochina wars, and fallout from the Cold War between the United States and the Soviet Union (and their respective allies.) At its core, acute conflict rose over North Vietnam's desire to unify the country under communist rule as modeled on the Soviet Union and China.

After France withdrew its rule from Indochina in 1954, Vietnam split into a communist North and anticommunist South, also populated by communist allies of the North known as Viet Cong. The growing conflict post-French occupation centered around the concept of communism and the threat of a full communist takeover of the peninsula. As the conflict progressed, US military advisers (and eventually personnel) joined with the South Vietnamese and other anticommunist allies, including troops from South Korea, Thailand, Australia, and New Zealand. On the other side, the Soviet Union and China poured weapons, supplies, and their own military advisers into the North, which was used to bolster Viet Cong campaign forces in the South.

PROJECT 1
TAKING SIDES

Set up a debate where half of your group represents the North and half South Vietnam, breaking down their main points.

- Choose a group of your peers to participate in this debate.
- Choose representatives to speak for the government in North Vietnam, the Viet Cong, the Soviet Union, and

To build your argument, make sure each member of your group represents a different party or nation in the coalition, and that each position is equally strong.

China. Research their position or positions in the war, answering the following question: What unites these forces, and what did they have to gain individually from participation in the conflict? Make sure to take notes, citing particular information and data along with their sources.

- On the other side, involve the voices of Southern Vietnamese anticommunists, South Koreans, Thai, Americans, and the Australian and New Zealand Army Corps (ANZAC) troops. Research their positions and note what they were fighting for. Make sure to take notes, citing particular information and data along with their sources.

- Set up a debate between both sides. Each side should have an equal amount of time to present their information, and then to respond to the other side.

- Once the debate has been presented, ask the class to weigh in. Whose side do they believe? Who would they fight for?

- If there is any division amongst the class, use this to explain the importance of exploring multiple perspectives and understanding across political lines.

QUESTION 2 HOW, WHY, AND WHEN DID WESTERN COUNTRIES SUCH AS THE UNITED STATES OF AMERICA BECOME INVOLVED IN THE VIETNAM WAR?

US military advisors were present in Vietnam in the 1950s, prior to French withdrawal from Vietnam. During this time, economic and military aid (noncombat only) was provided to deter the spread of communism in the peninsula. After France withdrew and Vietnam divided, the United States continued its support by sending advisors to Vietnam. This support increased annually, and escalated into the deployment of regular US combat troops beginning in 1965, following the Gulf of Tonkin incident in 1964.

On August 2, 1964, two North Vietnamese torpedo boats attacked USS *Maddox* in broad daylight in the Gulf of Tonkin,

Naval ships like this aircraft carrier, the USS *Coral Sea*, would have been a common sight in the Gulf of Tonkin in 1968.

where the US warship was gathering communications intelligence. Two nights later, USS *Maddox* and the destroyer USS *Turner Joy* reported that they were under attack. However, a nearby pilot did not notice any ships in the area where the torpedo boats were reported; years later, crew members admitted they had never seen an attacking craft. Purportedly, an electrical storm may have been interfering with the ships' radar, giving the impression of an approaching attack.

This alleged unprovoked incident sparked the Gulf of Tonkin Resolution, granting President Johnson full capacity to order American troops to invade Vietnam. After their deployment, other members of the Southeast Asia Treaty Organization (SEATO) and the Republic of South Vietnam joined forces against the spread of communism from the North.

PROJECT 2
BATTLESHIP REENACTMENT

Involve your class in a reenactment of what was purported to have happened in the Gulf of Tonkin between August 2 and 4, 1964—including the immediate reaction from the United States.

- Read "Case Closed: The Gulf of Tonkin Incident" by Captain Carl Otis Schuster, which can be found at http://www.historynet.com/case-closed-the-gulf-of-tonkin-incident.htm.
- Create a timeline of the purported events.
- With your class, enact the events listed on your timeline.
- Poll the class. Was it still "worth it" to escalate the war, if it was based on a lie? Is it ever OK for someone in charge (i.e. the president) to lie to his or her country in order

to drive a situation forward toward a mutually agreed upon outcome?

- Does this remind anyone in the class of tactics used to escalate US involvement in a subsequent war?
- Remind the class of the Iraq War, providing some knowledge of its impetus in the events of 9/11, if none is volunteered. How does this compare to the supposed events of the Gulf of Tonkin incident?

QUESTION 3 WHAT FACTORS LED TO THE WITHDRAWAL OF AMERICAN TROOPS FROM VIETNAM?

While direct US military involvement persisted until August 1973, the Tet Offensive marked a turning point in the war back in 1968, when US public confidence in the war was really shaken. On January 31, 1968, over 85,000 North Vietnamese forces launched an attack on five major South Vietnamese cities, dozens of military stations, and innumerable towns and villages in the South. By February of that year, death tolls had risen in Vietnam to over 500 per week. Between these numbers, media coverage of the war, and the antiwar movement emerging large and strong across the Western world, American citizens found themselves more and more dissatisfied by the limited progress that US war efforts seemed to be making. All of this put pressure on the Johnson administration and US Congress not to escalate the war effort.

However, this backlash came at odds to an upsurge in optimism felt by US military following the Tet Offensive. They believed they had successfully turned back the enemy and had weaked communist forces. As a result, angry US citizens and antiwar protestors had another five years to wait for removal of troops from Vietnam, after a long, bloody battle leading to defeat at the hands of the communist North. The Paris Peace Accord followed, signed January 1973, though removal of all US troops from Vietnam dragged on until 1975.

PROJECT 3
"VIETNAMIZATION": A POLICY

On March 22, 1968, General William C. Westmoreland was recalled to the United States to become chief of staff of the army and replaced by General Creighton Abrams, who pursued the Vietnamization program and began the reduction of the US presence in Vietnam to fewer than 30,000 troops.

- Outline President Nixon and chief adviser Henry Kissinger's six-step withdrawal plan (to avoid outright acceptance of "defeat" but still allowing US troops to get out of Vietnam).
- Use the medium of a short play to allow the class a window of access into the military strategy room. What time frame are you representing? Who is present in the room? What information were they using in their decision-making process? Choose an access point and make sure that your depiction is accurate.
- Follow the short play with a "debriefing," involving the class.
- What strategies did they see being utilized in the war room? Who could they identify, and what was their stance on the war and purpose for being there?

- Public outcry against the Vietnam War began in 1964 and escalated sharply in 1968, but troops were not fully withdrawn from the military zone in Vietnam until 1975, two years after the peace accord was signed. Why does the class think it took so long for the US government and military decision-making policies to match public opinion?

CHAPTER TWO

A CITIZEN'S CHOICE

Civics is the study of citizenship, its rights and duties. It includes both the rights of citizens to one another and to their government. All discussion of civics must involve the three main branches of government (executive, legislative, and judicial) and the US Constitution. It also incorporates the topics of politics and society, community participation, and civic virtue.

Civics relates to the Vietnam War and antiwar movement most directly as an example or expression of the political climate in the United States—and its generational

Some antiwar demonstrators chose to burn their draft cards in protest, as this man did in 1967.

divisions—spanning from the mid-1950s into the 1970s. This is a particularly generous segment of time in this nation's history, and it is bookended by major differences in public opinion toward the US government between the conservative, Cold War-driven 1950s and the more liberal counterculture of the late 1960s and 1970s. However, these tensions provided Americans with a legal platform to exercise their rights and duties as individual citizens under the support of their government.

FACTS ABOUT THE DRAFT

Before December 1969, conscription took place under the legal authority of a "peacetime" draft, as the United States did not ever formally declare war on North Vietnam. This was made legally possible by an act signed by President Franklin D. Roosevelt in 1940 in anticipation of mobilizing civilian-soldiers into World War II. According to the University of Michigan's Resistance and Revolution project, this type of draft inducted more than 1.4 million American men at an average of 120,000 per year between 1954 and 1964. In late July 1965, Johnson doubled the number of men to be drafted from 17,000 to 35,000 per month. On August 31, he signed a law making it a crime to burn a draft card.

In response to critics of the peacetime draft, the Selective Service System conducted two lottery drawings on December 1, 1969, to determine the order in which draft-eligible men (born 1944 to 1950) would be called to report for evaluation and possible conscription into the military. This method of draft lottery was conducted again in 1970, 1971, and 1972, before the draft was abolished in early 1973 and the signature of the Paris Peace Accords on January 27, 1973.

QUESTION 4 HOW DID THE GULF OF TONKIN RESOLUTION GRANT PRESIDENT JOHNSON WITH THE POWER TO LAUNCH ANY MILITARY ACTIONS HE DEEMED NECESSARY?

After supposedly unprovoked attacks on American warships on August 2 and 4, 1964, President Johnson put a resolution forward before the US Congress asking them to approve and support the decisions of the president, in his singular position as commander in chief, to take all necessary measures (including the use of conventional military force) in preventing further aggression and repelling any current attacks.

While not an official declaration of war, the resolution instead declared maintenance of international peace in Southeast Asia. It passed in both houses of Congress on August 7. This also served as the principal constitutional authorization for the escalation of the US military's involvement in the Vietnam War. According to the US Department of Defense, troops deployed in 1961 numbered 2,000, while they had multiplied to 16,5000 by 1964. But as the American public lost interest in the war, many members of Congress came to see the resolution as a way of giving the president a unilateral power to wage war. The resolution was repealed in 1970.

PROJECT 4
JOINT RESOLUTION

The Gulf of Tonkin Resolution granted the president the authority "to promote the maintenance of international peace and security in southeast Asia." In reality, the provision allowed

Your class can also view archival footage of President Johnson speaking on the Gulf of Tonkin incident, which is available to watch on YouTube.

Johnson to send regular troops to Vietnam, and this admission of power was (almost) unilaterally accepted by Senate and the House of Representatives. In this project, reenact the debate that occurred in the lead-up to the Gulf of Tonkin Resolution.

- Form a small group with your classmates.
- Read the "Tonkin Gulf Resolution" at ourdocuments.gov.
- Next read "Senate Debate on the Gulf of Tonkin Resolution" at alphahistory.com
- With your group, re-enact the discussion on the Congress floor on that day, August 5, 1964, for the class. Give them some background information regarding the Gulf of Tonkin incident, and what was being declared.
- Make sure you touch upon the following questions: Why, at that time, would representatives of the American citizens be so quick to agree to give away their power to the president? What kind of special circumstances would drive a person or group of people to that decision?
- Ask the class to weigh in. How would they have voted? What sort of powers would they give the current president—or take away from him—if they were able?

QUESTION 5 WHAT WAS THE TET OFFENSIVE AND HOW DID ITS OUTCOME AFFECT PUBLIC SUPPORT OF THE WAR?

The Tet Offensive, known as one of the largest military campaigns of the Vietnam War, was launched by the Communist North (Viet Cong and the People's Army of Vietnam, known as PAVN) on January 31, 1968. It consisted of a series of surprise attacks against the South, in order to break the stalemate between the troops. Viet Cong forces attacked thirteen cities in South Vietnam just before celebrations of their lunar new year would have begun. The next day, PAVN struck cities, towns, military bases, and government buildings throughout the South, including an attack on the US Embassy, adding up to over 120 attacks overall.

In retaliation, US and ARVN forces inflicted heavy losses on the Viet Cong. Neither side could declare the demonstration an outright "victory" at its end, but it did signify the beginning of a new phase in the war—one that the American public was not necessarily on board with. Despite many casualties, North Vietnam won an important strategic victory, marking a turning point in the war and the beginning of American troops' slow, eventual withdrawal from the region.

PROJECT 5
ANTIWAR DEMONSTRATION

The Tet Offensive was crucial in terms of provoking anger and unrest amongst the American people against the war. While designed to encourage the United States to scale back involvement in the war, the attacks largely bolstered the American military forces in power. However, news coverage of the offensive shocked the American public, leading to a severe loss in support for the war. In this project, you can involve your class with a recreation of an antiwar protest against the Vietnam War.

- Provide the class with materials for their exploration. You can stream YouTube video clips of the news media coverage of the Tet Offensive and/or provide newspaper clips keeping a tally of the casualties accumulating on both sides.

- Encourage classmates to absorb the information for themselves, as citizens might have in the 1960s. How would they interpret or process what they are seeing?
- Take a poll. Would the class agree they would have been against the war themselves?
- Lead a discussion with the class as to how this information would lead some Americans to take an antiwar position.
- Start a protest. Taking their opinions into consideration, get the class to come up with their own posters for an antiwar march. What are some good slogans they may have used or chosen for themselves in 1968?

QUESTION 6 WHY WAS THE ANTIWAR MOVEMENT SO STRONG DURING THE VIETNAM WAR?

At the peak of the antiwar movement, nearly a third of the American population was strongly and openly against the Vietnam War. The draft lottery became a large point of consideration as a basis for protest, in contrast with its initiation as a civic duty. In the eyes of many, the draft forced people too young to drink or vote to risk their lives for a war "no one" believed in. Many people also realized that those in the poorer classes and racial minorities were more likely to get chosen for the draft than others. This led to extreme reactions against the practice.

While the movement began as an isolated issue among students and Cold War oppositionists, the war's expansion in 1965 widened its pool of opposition, and shed light on those already politically active against the Vietnam War. Peace groups were eager to educate the public and the press regarding their open opposition. The lynchpin was in normalizing this sentiment, and the deeper America dove into the messy war post-1965, the easier this became. Popular politicians such as Senator Robert Kennedy were solidly antiwar, as were popular young figures such as Muhammad Ali. Many were willing to copy their habits, engaging in nonviolent civil disobedience. After the Tet offensive and other violent escalations on both sides, such as intensified bombing set in motion by President Nixon, both physical retaliation in Vietnam and antiwar fervor at home began to appeal more.

A group of students stand in peaceful protest of the draft and the Vietnam War in Washington, DC, in 1965.

PROJECT 6
INTRODUCING THE DRAFT

Conscription in the United States, popularly known as the draft, has been used by the federal government of the United States in four conflicts: the American Civil War; World War I; World War II; and the Cold War, which includes both the Korean War and the Vietnam War. In this project, engage your class in a modern-day conscription, drawing names to demonstrate who goes to war and who stays at home.

After your presentation, make sure to ask your classmates for their thoughts, and engage them in a discussion related to your topic.

- Using data from the Selective Service System and the National Archives, research information about who was drafted during the Vietnam War. Were more people from a particular racial or socioeconomic group drafted than others? If so, why? Were there any avenues for American men to legally get out of the draft? What were they? How did this affect who was represented in the draft?
- Create a presentation using a tool such as PowerPoint about the Vietnam War draft and who it affected.
- Ask students to write down their thoughts regarding the use of the draft during the Vietnam War. Is it a duty of all Americans? Was it unfair or unjust in any way? How did it contribute to the way Americans viewed their patriotic duties or their reaction to the Vietnam War?
- Ask the class to share their thoughts in a discussion. You can bring the topic of discussion to the modern day, asking whether or not there any obvious benefits to enforcing voluntary armed forces for Americans even today.

CHAPTER THREE

OVER LAND AND SEA

Geographical study demands a focus on physical and human-made features across the surface of the Earth, including distributions of landforms and bodies of water, and the locations of places and regions, including shifting political boundaries. Those engaged in the study of geography

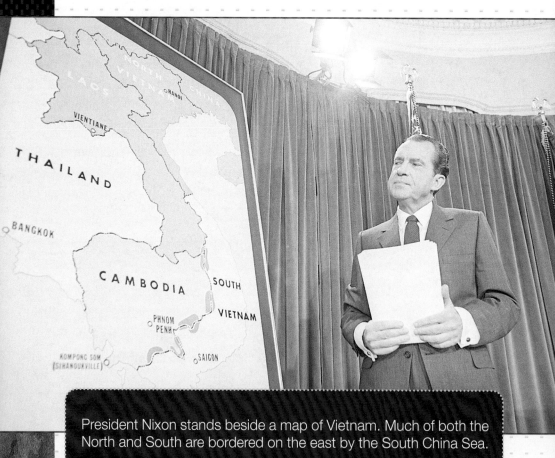

President Nixon stands beside a map of Vietnam. Much of both the North and South are bordered on the east by the South China Sea.

are generally interested in both spatial and environmental perspectives, through the use of maps.

Geography played an immense part in shaping the Vietnam War, both at home in America and in the theater of war in Vietnam. Studying the geography of Vietnam was essential for military personnel as they strategized and fought in the war. And while the war remained thousands of miles away in Vietnam, media advances such as the television brought the realities of the war into the American home.

SEARCH AND DESTROY

For the first time during the Vietnam War, search and destroy was deployed as a method of warfare via the use of a new piece of aerial technology: the helicopter. Because of the geographical complexity of the jungles of Vietnam, the traditional methods of "taking ground" useful in previous wars fought by American military could not be used in this war. This would be a new kind of war, in which the enemy would be eliminated by "searching" for them and then "destroying" them; the "body count" would be the tool they used to determine whether or not they had been successful.

QUESTION 7 WHAT IS GUERILLA WARFARE, AND HOW DOES IT COMPARE TO MORE CONVENTIONAL STYLES OF WAR? HOW WAS IT USED IN THE VIETNAM WAR?

Vietnam as a whole is made up of tropical lowlands and forested highlands. Level land only makes up approximately 20 percent of the area. The impact of jungles, mountains, and heavy rainfall made a great difference toward the successes and failures amassed during the Vietnam War, on both sides.

As natives to the South, the Viet Cong were more comfortable within its geographical layout than their own Northern allies or the invading troops, and thus fought a guerrilla-style war against the anti-communist forces in the region. The People's Army of Vietnam, also known as the North Vietnamese Army (NVA), on the other hand, engaged in more conventional warfare, at times committing large units to battle.

PROJECT 7
WELCOME TO THE JUNGLE

Consider the mindset of a Viet Cong soldier. They would have been familiar with Vietnam's geography—its landforms and rivers, as well as any changes in political boundaries—than most others involved in the strategic side of the war. They would have been quick to employ guerilla tactics rather than relying upon slower, more traditional army units. But how did the land of Southern Vietnam itself have an effect on their approach?

- Create a presentation with a geographical map of Vietnam and photos of the jungles and mountains from the war era.
- Make sure to include the following questions in your presentation: How were geographical features used by the Viet Cong to "gain ground" and keep their advantage? How did geography affect American troops?
- How might geography change the tactics used by both sides in the war? Ask the class to consider tactics such as ambushes, sabotage, raids, petty warfare, and

Looking at maps helps us to conceptualize, or better visualize, important events in history.

hit-and-run to fight a large and more traditional army. Define any key words that are not familiar to the class.

- Finally, ask the class about how geographical features might be "overcome" with new technologies. What technologies did American troops use in the Vietnam War to aid them in this terrain? What contemporary technology might be used in wars in the present day?

QUESTION 8 WHAT EFFECTS MUST GEOGRAPHY HAVE ON HOW WAR IS CONDUCTED IN A SPECIFIC REGION OR COUNTRY?

Wars are not fought haphazardly, nor are they generally decided in a single battle. The Vietnam War lasted twenty years, with American martial engagement spanning nearly a decade. It is possible to study military strategy at university, and graduate with

These captured Viet Cong knew a lot more about their native terrain in South Vietnam than the American soldiers did when they first arrived.

degrees specializing in war tactics. These people decide where and how battles are fought, and how best to organize troops, minimize casualties, and gain ground—amongst other important goals. In this way, fighting in a field would require a very different strategy than fighting in a forest, jungle, or at sea.

From the outset, one would need to consider visibility, the concept of "higher ground," and how best to utilize different branches of the military—including the Army, Navy, Marines, and Air Force. Vietnam presented a challenging arena for battle to even the most hardened of strategists and combat soldiers. With a variety of land features spanning low-lying river beds to soaring mountain ranges, densely covered areas of jungle, and a grueling tropical climate, Vietnam introduced challenges the American soldier had not faced during any prior war, on American or European soil.

PROJECT 8
THE LAY OF THE LAND

Introduce the class to the varied theater of the Vietnam War through a slideshow presentation and discussion.

- Research "hot spots" during the Vietnam War, where there was active fighting. Where did warfare occur and what strategies were used during these battles? Make sure to include a variety of areas, including urban, rural, and maritime.
- Create a slideshow of photos of these varied geographical areas, using a program like Scoompa Video.
- Present your slideshow to the class, giving them a sense of the landscape and climate of Vietnam. Ask them the following questions: Are they surprised by its most prominent features? What did they expect?

Photographs of Vietnam's terrain show a level of detail that a simple map is not designed to do. It is important to use both when forming a battle strategy.

- Divide the class in thirds. Have one group strategize a battle at sea, another negotiate an urban arena, and a third approach engaging battle in a rural setting. Bring examples of designs and tactics to share for brainstorming purposes.
- Ask the class to demonstrate their strategies. How do they differ, and what remains the same across all three? What, if anything, did they prioritize? How much of their considerations depended on differences in geography? What, if any, other factors required them to change their tactics?

ECONOMY OF WAR

Economics deals with the knowledge of human capital, land, investments, money, income and production, taxes, and government spending. As a field of study, it covers the distribution of capital and natural resources, the consideration for costs versus benefits, buyers and sellers, and a national economy.

As an aspect of social studies, economics can be a useful lens for discussion of social class and the allocation of resources during wartime. During the Vietnam War and the antiwar movement in the United States of America, class differences were particularly divisive in terms of separating those who could afford to dodge the war—or at the very least, lead it. Soldiers in Vietnam were often poor young men, with lower class backgrounds, and no idea how to cope. When these men started to return home traumatized, addicted to drugs, and unable to assimilate

Many Vietnam War veterans returned ill equipped to handle the transition between life as a soldier and civilian. Without the resources in place, many suffered from homelessness.

into American society, larger portions of the population were forced to question what was really going on in Vietnam, and how these soldiers were being treated (or not) by their own government.

BODY COUNT

During the Vietnam War, body count became a focus not only for military strategists but the daily media in televised news coverage of the war. Body count was used as a measure of productivity, progress, and success—the idea being that the count for American and other Allied troops should be low while Northern Vietnamese troops should be high. In this kind of war, all contested territory was already held, in theory. Therefore, progress was measured in people—bodies killed, rather than land seized.

Estimates of the casualties incurred during the Vietnam War vary greatly, even to this day. The Vietnamese government reported 849,018 NVA/NLF combatants died during the war, while 58,220 Americans and approximately 313,000 South Vietnamese combatants were killed in the conflict. The official US Department of Defense (DOD) figure states that 950,765 communist forces were eliminated in Vietnam from 1965 to 1974. Currently, DOD analysts believe these figures need to be deflated by thirty percent.

QUESTION 9 HOW DID CLASS AND RACE FACTOR INTO THE DRAFT DURING THE VIETNAM WAR?

The draft system in place in America in 1967 called as many as 40,000 men for induction into the military each month. This draft seemed to favor white, middle-class men while economically and racially discriminating against minority ethnic groups. Young African-American men, in particular, found themselves serving at disproportionately higher rates than the rest of the population in general. According to author Herman Graham III, in 1967 64 percent of black men were selected in the draft, while only 31 percent of eligible white men were drafted that year.

Draft card burning was used as a symbol of protest by thousands of young men across America during the late 1960s and early 1970s. Historically, the first draft card burners on record in the United States were actively opposed to US involvement in the Vietnam War. The first publicized protest took place in December 1963 when a conscientious objector named Eugene Keyes set fire to his card on Christmas Day in Illinois. A larger, organized demonstration followed in May 1964, when in Union Square, New York City, about fifty participants burned their cards.

PROJECT 9
AVOIDING THE DRAFT

Invite the class to take part in a draft card "burning" (participation optional), in which they are all given draft cards to serve in the Vietnam War.

- **Look up what Vietnam era-draft cards looked like, and attempt to replicate them. Make one card for each of your classmates.**
- **After handing out draft cards, lead the class in a discussion of who would have likely burned their draft cards and who would not have.**

- Ask your classmates to "burn" their draft cards by ripping them up, or deciding not to "burn" them.
- Did anyone in the class choose not to burn their cards? Invite them to share why. Invite some early discussion as to why some may have chosen to burn them while others said no.

- Ask the class to consider other ways in which men and boys avoided the draft. Consider pre-emptive measures such as enrolling in university, and through demonstrations afterward such as burning their cards or faking mental or physical illness during their fitness examinations. How would these ways out of the war favor wealthy and privileged white Americans?
- Consider the economic advantage for boys and men with families who could afford to send their children to college, versus those at the other end of the spectrum whose families might need their financial support after leaving school.

Consider the war from another's perspective. While avoiding the draft might seem simple to you today, for many at the time compliance was nonnegotiable.

QUESTION 10 CONSIDER THE NEWS MEDIA AS "BUYERS AND SELLERS" OF WAR. WHERE ARE THEY GETTING THEIR INFORMATION FROM, AND HOW ARE THEY CHOOSING TO BEST DISTRIBUTE—AND SLANT—IT?

The Vietnam War was the first widely televised war. While the seeds of this technology and its American audience were planted during the Korean War, they were not quite there on a large enough scale. The first "living-room war," a term coined by Michael Arlen, brought reporters from the battlefield to the five o'clock news. Gone were the days where foreign correspondents had to rely on print media to bring their stories to life; now, cameras could

Foreign war correspondents (journalists and photographers) captured key moments in the day-to-day realities of the war, such as this evacuation of Vietnamese civilians.

be placed within war zones to capture footage from the front. While still a far cry from the pace demanded from online news media today, television, radio, and print journalism allowed for daily changes to the war efforts in the form of the draft lottery, body count, and other important and ongoing updates.

Lowered censorship allowed for by this new media exploded into antiwar sentiment in some, and a larger sense of patriotism in others. In both cases, a war abroad was brought home in the most tangible way conceivable at that time; in 1965, Lyndon Johnson criticized the TV news network CBS for its depiction of a report by Morley Safer in which Marines set fire to a village of civilians in South Vietnam. But by no means was this standard fare for televised broadcast. Most news from the war was contained, and did not contain images of a graphic nature; it was only during the 1968 Tet and 1972 Spring offensives, which were fought in urban areas, that the violence and suffering produced by the war was shown more regularly on television.

PROJECT 10
MEDIA ECONOMICS

Despite what many may think, the relationship between television news programming or newspapers and their viewers is largely economic. News outlets rely on revenue from both advertising and sales in order to pay their journalists, and to bring the news to their audience. In this project, explore how these economic realities affected reporting on the Vietnam War.

- Read "Vietnam: A Censored War" by John A. Cloud, as featured on the *Harvard Crimson* website.
- Find video clips online of American reporting of the Vietnam War.

Consider the American public at the time of the Vietnam War. What would they have made of the style of reporting that occurs now online and through social media?

- Present these clips to your class, and distribute "Vietnam: A Censored War."
- Ask the class how the American media reported on the Vietnam War. Were the realities of the war censored or uncensored? Why or why not?
- Think through the economics of the media. Why would a television station or newspaper decide to censor the graphic nature of the war? What economic motivators may have led news outlets to report the Vietnam War in a specific way?
- Next, ask your class if they think newspapers should report everything they see, or if they should rather be concerned with their bottom line and their audience. Ask your classmates to explain their response.

CHAPTER FIVE

AFTERMATH AND HEALING

Three similar fields of study—anthropology, psychology, and sociology—can equally be related to social studies. Anthropology is the scientific study of humans as they appear or have appeared in societies across the globe, drawing on social, natural, and physical sciences and the humanities (which generally refers to literature, philosophy, and the arts). Psychology is the study of the mind and human behavior, while sociology is the study of the social lives of people, groups, and societies. One will notice that there is a fair amount of overlap between these three fields; their focus as a whole is very much on people and their workings, both internally and as part of a larger society.

Wartime and its surrounding efforts have afforded psychologists, anthropologists, and sociologists with quite a bit of fodder for analysis. In this way, the Vietnam War and its subsequent antiwar movement have drawn historians to filter their view through these lenses. Perhaps the easiest lens to access, but the hardest to fix, has been psychology. According to psychologist Charles Marmar, post-traumatic

This American soldier can be seen firing an M16 rifle during the My Lai massacre in 1968, perceived by many to be the most shocking and upsetting event of the war.

stress disorder (PTSD) continues to affect approximately 11 percent of American men who served in the Vietnam War— over 200,000 veterans—more than forty years after troops were brought home. Additionally, more than one third of these vets have a concurrent diagnosis of major depressive disorder. By studying these mental health cases and other issues, current psychologists and psychiatrists can hope to reduce these statistics in veterans stationed in Iraq and Afghanistan.

UNITED FRONT FOR THE LIBERATION OF OPPRESSED RACES (FULRO)

While many textbooks about the Vietnam War tend to cluster all South Vietnamese together into one demographic in opposition to a united North Vietnam and the Viet Cong, there are several minority ethnic populations in South Vietnam, such as the Christian Montagnards, who are native to the highlands and ethnically distinct from the lowland Vietnamese. Around the time of the Vietnam War, the Montagnards began to rebel against the South Vietnamese lowlanders, who they viewed as colonialists intent on taking their land and changing their way of life. With others, including the Hindu and Muslim Cham and the Buddhist Khmer Krom, the Montagnards banded together to create the United Front for the Liberation of Oppressed Races (FULRO), to fight against the Vietnamese for independence.

American forces worked with FULRO during the war as reconnaissance units. Orders were to remain disengaged from infighting among the ethnic groups, but it was easy for American soldiers to support FULRO, as the Montagnards protected them and kept them safe in the jungle. Their position as an ethnic minority group fighting for recognition and freedom also made sense to many young Americans who were supportive of the civil rights movement at home in the United States.

QUESTION 11 ANY DISCUSSION OF THE VIETNAM WAR BRINGS TO MIND A SENSE OF BRUTALITY AND THE COMMITMENT OF UNSPEAKABLE ACTS, ON BOTH SIDES. WHAT WERE SOME OF THE WORST WAR CRIMES COMMITTED DURING THE VIETNAM WAR?

While many might consider extreme acts of violence toward civilians and prisoners of war such as rape, massacre, bombing, terrorism, torture, and murder to be obvious war crimes, common crimes such as theft, arson, and property destruction can also be committed as acts of wartime destruction. It is also important to remember that war crimes are committed on both sides during times of war.

The Khmer Rouge army was a name given to Cambodian, or Khmer, communists built up in the jungles in Eastern Cambodia during the late 1960s and supported by the army in North Korea and the Viet Cong. They were known for their harsh treatment of anyone they saw as a political opponent, including murdering between 1.5 and 3 million citizens during the Cambodian genocide following the Cambodian Civil War. In South Vietnam, however, the anti-communist troops were far from blameless. The My Lai massacre of 1968 claimed the lives of between 350 and 500 unarmed Vietnamese citizens at the hands of US soldiers; these men, women, and children were all killed, and many women were raped and mutilated. This massacre has been deemed "the most shocking episode of the Vietnam War." When investigative journalists uncovered the extent of the tragedy, the American public was outraged.

PROJECT 11
ANALYSIS OF MY OWN CRIMES

Crimes (or bad behavior of any kind) can be committed by anyone, irrespective of their positioning as "good" or "evil." While Americans were anticommunist and would have considered themselves on the side of "good," their behavior during the Vietnam War was certainly not without fault, between falsification of the conditions for entering the war, via the Gulf of Tonkin incident, and the "shocking" criminal behavior that took place

Consider yourself on your worst day. Is it easy to justify your behavior? What might drive an otherwise sane person to commit acts he or she would normally think of as unlawful?

during the My Lai massacre. In this project, discuss with your class how normal people can be compelled to commit extreme acts under pressure, particularly during times of war.

- Research a war crime committed by either side during the Vietnam War.
- Note how people involved in the crime spoke about their actions, and whether or not they attempted to excuse their own behavior or if they faced consequences.
- Compile your findings into a presentation, which you can share with your class.
- Ask your class the following questions: How should governments deal with war crimes? Who should be punished? Should "bad behavior" during wartime ever be excused if the reasoning were tactical? What, if anything, differentiates killing the opposition's military personnel, versus targeting "innocent" civilians?
- Ask the class to consider the "worst thing they've ever done."
- Direct the class to complete a writing exercise in which they discuss their crime, and any punishment (self-inflicted or by others) they suffered for it. If there are volunteers, they can share their experiences.

QUESTION 12 HOW AND WHY DID PSYCHOLOGICAL DISTURBANCE BECOME SO WIDESPREAD AMONGST SOLDIERS DURING THE VIETNAM WAR? HOW DID THE WAR AFFECT THE STUDY AND TREATMENT OF PTSD?

Mental wellness was not generally a topic for widespread discussion in the 1960s. At this time, physical illness and mental

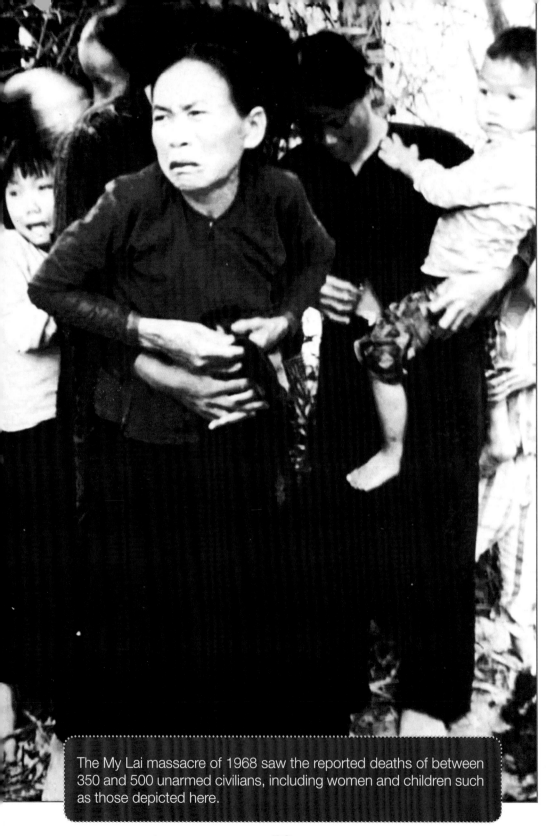

The My Lai massacre of 1968 saw the reported deaths of between 350 and 500 unarmed civilians, including women and children such as those depicted here.

illness were not seen as equal in the eyes of many Americans; in fact, mental illness would have suggested fragility and delicacy in men, whereas many women were still seen as hysterical and sent to hospital. However, the unusual circumstances of the war—drug use at the front, not to mention exposure to Agent Orange, the average age and experience of soldiers, the unfamiliar terrain, and repercussions of protest and disillusionment at home—led to a severe lack of enthusiasm from the troops. This manifested in more measurable after effects, including rising rates of homelessness, post-traumatic stress disorder, and even suicide.

PROJECT 12
THE THINGS THEY CARRIED

In this project, you can use "The Things They Carried," a short story written by Tim O'Brien, as a starting place to discuss literature as a force against mental illness for people experiencing war firsthand.

- Read the short story "The Things They Carried." What references to mental illness are there in this text? How are these examples of mental illness dealt with?
- Share the story with your class.
- Analyze this text with the class. What is the difference between fiction and memoir? Is it important to differentiate between the two, or can fiction be just as "true" (or, at least as powerful) as fact? Why might a veteran turn to fiction to tell a story of war and mental illness?

QUESTION 13 WHAT WAS SO APPEALING ABOUT THE ANTIWAR MOVEMENT IN AMERICA THAT CAUSED ITS GENERAL TRENDINESS, ENCOURAGING A COUNTERCULTURE OF HIPPIES THAT CARRIED INTO THE LATE 1970S—LONGER THAN THE WAR ITSELF?

A counterculture is the culture of a group of typically young people whose values and lifestyles are considerably different to those of the established culture. After a period of growth, its peak and decline may be rapid, but its effects on the mainstream culture and its values are often long lasting. The hippie counterculture that supported the antiwar movement was highly influenced by the bohemian movement that began in 1850 and has been linked with the nomadic Romani people who migrated to France from the kingdom of Bohemia. Bohemians typically espoused communal living, sexual freedom, creativity, and sharing of resources.

Like the bohemians that came before them, the hippies of the 1960s shared a distrust of government, a notion of free love, and the desire for sexual and individual freedom. Taking the movement to its furthest, some hippies were considered communists themselves, and even flew the Viet Cong flag in protest of the war.

One product of the hippie counterculture and of the 1960s was the American rock musical *Hair*. In fact, many of its songs became anthems for the antiwar movement itself. A controversial production depicting a multiracial cast and involving nudity, sexuality, profanity, and drugs, *Hair* tells the story of a group young, politically-minded hippies as they live in New York City and fight against being drafted into the Vietnam War. For many young people in the 1960s, the antiwar movement became part of a larger trend and lifestyle that revolved around questioning authority and seeking personal freedom.

PROJECT 13
THE DAWNING OF THE AGE OF AQUARIUS

Engage the class in a read along from a pivotal scene in *Hair*, analyzing the cultural and social trends of this moment in time.

- Choose an important scene in *Hair* that demonstrates the countercultural moment.
- Bring in copies of the scene for your classmates, and choose a classmate for each role.
- Read through the scene.
- Ask the class what important social and cultural issues appear in this scene. What can this scene teach us about this group of people living at this moment in time?
- Now extend your discussion. Why does hippie culture— and the idea of a "counterculture" in general—continue to appeal to young people today? Is hippie culture particularly American? Why or why not? How might countercultural movements in other cultures be different?

GLOSSARY

ABROAD Beyond the boundaries of one's country; in or to a foreign country.

AMBUSH To attack by surprise from a hidden place.

COMBAT Active military fighting during wartime.

COMMUNISM An economic system in which goods are owned and are available to everyone, meaning there is no private property; a totalitarian system of government based in Marxist theory in which a single political party controls all state-owned production, and economic goods are distributed evenly.

COMMUNIST An adherent or advocate of communism, through support of and engagement with a Communist government, party, or movement.

CONSCIENTIOUS OBJECTOR A person who refuses to serve in the armed forces or bear arms on moral or religious grounds.

CONSCRIPTION The compulsory enrollment of groups of people for military service; the draft.

CONSERVATIVE Favoring a policy of keeping things as they are, as opposed to change; favoring established styles and standards.

COUNTERCULTURE A subculture with defining values and customs that run against those of the established society.

DEPLOYMENT To arrange in appropriate positions for a deliberate purpose, such as in battle formation.

GUERILLA A member of a usually small group of soldiers who engages in irregular warfare, carrying out harassment and sabotage, especially as a member of an independent unit who does not belong to a regular army.

HIPPIE Generally, a young person who rejects the values of traditional society (as by dressing unconventionally or by living communally) and does not believe, and thus fights against, war.

MARTIAL Relating to an army or to the military.

MOBILITY The quality or capacity to be mobile; ability to move.

PENINSULA A portion of land surrounded mostly by water but still connected to a larger body by way of an isthmus.

RECONNAISSANCE A preliminary survey to gain information; for example, a military survey of enemy territory prior to the battle itself.

SABOTAGE Deliberate obstructive or destructive action carried on by civilian or enemy agents to hinder a nation's war effort.

STALEMATE A conflict or contest in which neither side can gain an advantage or win.

SUBSEQUENT Happening or coming after something else; following in time, order, or place.

FOR MORE INFORMATION

American Legion
700 North Pennsylvania Street
PO Box 1055
Indianapolis, IN 46206
(317) 630-1200
Website: https://www.legion.org
Facebook: @americanlegionhq
Twitter: @AmericanLegion
Instagram: @theamericanlegion
YouTube: @americanlegionHQ
The American Legion was chartered by Congress in 1919 as a veterans organization. It is the nation's largest veterans service organization, and it works toward mentoring youth, advocating for veterans' rights, and promoting national security.

American Veterans (AMVETS)
4647 Forbes Boulevard
Lanham, MD 20706
(877) 726-8387
Website: http://amvets.org
Facebook: @AMVETSHQ
Twitter: @AMVETSNational
YouTube: @AMVETSnational
Since 1944 AMVETS has provided support for veterans and the active military. It works to help procure entitlements for military members and advocates for reform that enhances

the quality of life of citizens and veterans alike. AMVETS is one of the largest veterans' service organizations in the United States.

The American Veterans Heritage Center (AVHC)
Building 120
4100 W Third Street
Dayton, OH 45428
(937) 267-7628
Website: http://www.americanveteransheritage.org
The American Veterans Heritage Center is a nonprofit corporation that seeks to honor the accomplishments of veterans. It also preserves the historic Soldiers Home, located in Dayton, Ohio.

Canadian Vietnam Veterans Association
813 Nottingham Avenue
Winnipeg, Manitoba
Canada R2K 2C9
(204) 668-8774
Website: http://www.cvva.ca
The Canadian Vietnam Veterans Association aids Vietnam War veterans who served in the Canadian or US Armed Forces. One of their largest achievements was obtaining medical benefits for veterans in Canada.

Disabled American Veterans (DAV)
3725 Alexandria Pike
Cold Spring, KY 41076
(877) 426-2838
Website: https://www.dav.org

Facebook: @The.DAV

Twitter: @davhq

Disabled American Veterans empowers veterans to live with respect and dignity. The organization works to make sure veterans and their families can access all the benefits entitled to them and educates the public about the sacrifices and needs of veterans returning back to civilian life.

Vietnam Veterans Memorial Fund (VVMF)

1235 South Clark Street, Suite 910

Arlington, VA 22202

(202) 393-0090

Website: http://www.vvmf.org

Facebook: @VietnamVeteransMemorialFund

Twitter: @VVMF

The Vietnam Veterans Memorial Fund is the nonprofit organization authorized by the US Congress to build a national memorial dedicated to all US service members in the Vietnam War.

Vietnam Veterans of America (VVA)

8719 Colesville Road, Suite 100

Silver Spring, MD 20910

(301) 585-4000

Website: https://vva.org

Facebook: @VietnamVeteransofAmerica

Twitter: @VVAmerica

The Vietnam Veterans of American work to change public perception of Vietnam veterans, as well as supporting a wide range of issues that affect Vietnam veterans.

FOR FURTHER READING

Burgan, Michael. T*he Vietnam War: An Interactive Modern History Adventure* (You Choose Books). North Mankato, MA: Capstone Press, 2014.

Freedman, Russell. *Vietnam: A History of the War*. New York: Holiday House, 2016.

Killcoyne, Hope Lourie, ed. *Key Figures of the Vietnam War* (Biographies of War). New York: Britannica Educational Publishing, 2016.

McNab, Chris. *50 Things You Should Know About the Vietnam War.* Lake Forest, CA: QEB Publishing, Inc., 2016.

Metzenthen, David. *Dreaming the Enemy*. Sydney: A & U Children, 2016.

Murray, Stuart. *Vietnam War* (DK Eyewitness Books). New York: DK, 2017.

O'Connor, Sheila. *Until Tomorrow, Mr. Marsworth*. New York: G. P. Putnam's Sons, 2018.

Otfinoski, Steven. *The Vietnam War* (Step into History). New York: Scholastic, 2017.

Schmermund, Elizabeth. *Minority Soldiers Fighting in the Vietnam War* (Fighting for Their Country). New York: Cavendish Square, 2018.

Small, Cathleen. *Strategic Inventions of the Vietnam War* (Tech in the Trenches). New York: Cavendish Square, 2016.

Steele, Philip. *Did Anything Good Come Out of the Vietnam War?* (Innovation Through Adversity). New York: Rosen, 2016.

BIBLIOGRAPHY

Alperstein, Ben. "How Park Chung-hee Made the Most of the South Korea-US Vietnam War Alliance." E-International Relations Students, July 9, 2017. http://www.e-ir .info/2017/07/09/how-park-chung-hee-made-the-most -of-the-south-korea-us-vietnam-war-alliance.

Barringer, Mark. "The Anti-War Movement in the United States." University of Illinois. Retrieved April 24, 2018. http://www .english.illinois.edu/maps/vietnam/antiwar.html.

Chickering, William H. "A War of Their Own." *New York Times*, June 9, 2017. https://www.nytimes.com/2017/06/09/opinion /a-war-of-their-own.html.

Cohen, Jeff, and Norman Solomon. "30-Year Anniversary: Tonkin Gulf Lie Launched Vietnam War." FAIR, July 27, 1994. https:// fair.org/media-beat-column/30-year-anniversary-tonkin -gulf-lie-launched-vietnam-war.

Ellsberg, Daniel. "Why the Pentagon Papers Matter Now." *Guardian*, June 14, 2011. https://www.theguardian.com /commentisfree/cifamerica/2011/jun/13/pentagon-papers -daniel-ellsberg.

Guttenplan, DD. "When Presidents Lie to Make a War." *Guardian*, August 2, 2014. https://www.theguardian.com /commentisfree/2014/aug/02/vietnam-presidents-lie -to-wage-war-iraq.

Hallin, Daniel. "Vietnam on Television." The Museum of Broadcast Communications. Retrieved April 24, 2018. http://www .museum.tv/eotv/vietnamonte.htm.

Kelly, Martin. "American Involvement in Wars from Colonial Times to the Present." *ThoughtCo*, March 3, 2018. https://www.thoughtco.com/american-involvement-wars-colonial-times-present-4059761.

Michigan in the World. "The Military Draft During the Vietnam War." University of Michigan. Retrieved March 26, 2018. http://michiganintheworld.history.lsa.umich.edu/antivietnamwar/exhibits/show/exhibit/draft_protests/the-military-draft-during-the-.

National Institute of Mental Health. "Post-Traumatic Stress Disorder." US Department of Health and Human Services February 2016. https://www.nimh.nih.gov/health/topics/post-traumatic-stress-disorder-ptsd/index.shtml.

Oaklander, Mandy. "More Than 200,000 Vietnam Vets Still Have PTSD." *Time*, July 22, 2015. http://time.com/3967590/vietnam-veterans-ptsd.

Taylor, Adam. "Why the World Should Not Forget Khmer Rouge and the Killing Fields of Cambodia." *Washington Post*, August 7, 2014. https://www.washingtonpost.com/news/worldviews/wp/2014/08/07/why-the-world-should-not-forget-khmer-rouge-and-the-killing-fields-of-cambodia.

Valentine, Tom. "Vietnam War Draft." The Vietnam War, May 9, 2016. https://thevietnamwar.info/vietnam-war-draft.

The White House. "Lyndon B. Johnson." WhiteHouse.gov. Retrieved March 26, 2018. https://www.whitehouse.gov/about-the-white-house/presidents/lyndon-b-johnson.

Zimmerman, Bill. "The Four Stages of the Antiwar Movement." *New York Times*, October 24, 2017. https://www.nytimes.com/2017/10/24/opinion/vietnam-antiwar-movement.html.

INDEX

ABOUT THE AUTHOR

Carolyn DeCarlo is a poet and fiction writer from Baltimore, Maryland, who now lives in New Zealand. She has written several chapbooks, including *Green Place* (Enjoy Journal, 2015). She has a BA in English and psychology from Georgetown University and an MFA in creative writing from the University of Maryland, College Park. She has studied the Vietnam War in depth at Georgetown University and the counterculture movement of the Beat poets at the University of Maryland. She was very pleased to return to this material for this textbook.

PHOTO CREDITS

Cover Tim Page/Corbis Historical/Getty Images; cover banner and interior pages (camouflage) cornflower/Shutterstock.com; p. 7 Paul Schutzer/The LIFE Picture Collection/Getty Images; p. 9 Terry Fincher/Hulton Archive/Getty Images; p. 11 Keystone /Hulton Archive/Getty Images; p. 13 Maskot/Getty Images; p. 15 MPI/Archive Photos/Getty Images; pp. 20, 30 Bettmann /Getty Images; p. 23 fstop123/E+/Getty Images; p. 27 Michael Ochs Archives/Getty Images; p. 28 Stretch Photography/Blend Images/Getty Images; pp. 33, 48 Hero Images/Getty Images; p. 34 ullstein bild/Getty Images; p. 36 Lumina Images/Blend Images/Getty Images; p. 37 Andrew Holbrooke/Corbis Historical /Getty Images; p. 40 John & Lisa Merrill/Photodisc/Getty Images; p. 41 Dominique Berretty/Gamma-Rapho/Getty Images; p. 43 Mark Edward Atkinson/Blend Images/Getty Images; p. 45 Ronald S. Haeberle/The LIFE Images Collection/Getty Images; p. 50 Universal Images Group/Getty Images.

Design and Layout: Nicole Russo-Duca; Editor and Photo Researcher: Elizabeth Schmermund